52 Weeks of
Self Reflection

Erika R. Dawkins

ISBN:0692730958
ISBN-13:9780692730959

Introduction

Self reflection is the effort made to take an effective look inside ourselves. Self reflection is a necessity.

Whether it be to move forward from something, prepare for something or understand something. Knowing who we are, how we manage life, and the impact we have on others, helps us become more self aware in the parts of our lives that need the most attention.

The next 52 weeks will open your eyes and ask questions you may not have asked yourself before. Be transparent and discover yourself through self reflection.

Dedication

This is dedicated to the little boy that made self reflection a requirement for my life, in order to provide a better one for him.

Week 1
Self-Image

What does self image mean to you?

_____

_____

_____

_____

_____

_____

_____

_____

_____

_____

_____

_____

_____

_____

_____

_____

_____

_____

_____

What 10 words best describe how you see yourself and why?

_____

_____

_____

_____

_____

_____

_____

_____

_____

_____

_____

_____

_____

_____

_____

_____

_____

Week 2

Friendship

How do you view friendship?

_____

_____

_____

_____

_____

_____

_____

_____

Do you consider yourself a good friend?

_____

_____

_____

_____

_____

_____

_____

_____

Do you have any friendships that have ended, that could have been saved? Discuss them.

_____

_____

_____

_____

_____

_____

_____

_____

Are you fulfilled in your friendships? If not, what do you need?

_____

_____

_____

_____

_____

_____

_____

_____

Week 3
Honesty with Self

Honesty with self can be difficult. It requires you to hold yourself accountable for bad decisions and to pat yourself on the back for good decisions. Both of these can be challenging at times.

Discuss times you made a great decision that made an impact on you or someone else that you have kept to yourself.

_____

_____

_____

_____

_____

_____

_____

_____

_____

Discuss times you made a bad decision and what the fall out was as a result of it.

_____

_____

_____

_____

_____

_____

_____

_____

_____

_____

_____

_____

_____

_____

_____

_____

_____

_____

_____

Week 4

Family

What does family mean to you?

_____

_____

_____

_____

_____

_____

_____

_____

_____

_____

_____

_____

_____

_____

_____

_____

_____

_____

Do you have healthy relationships with your family?

_____

_____

_____

_____

_____

_____

_____

_____

What can you do to make your family structure stronger?

_____

_____

_____

_____

_____

_____

_____

Week 5
Relationships

Relationships can be tricky sometimes. Some are good experiences and others are not. Discuss what relationships mean to you and express some of the strong and weak points of past relationships. You may also discuss some things you would have handled differently.

_____

_____

_____

_____

_____

_____

_____

_____

_____

_____

_____

Week 6

Happiness

What does happiness mean to you?

_____

_____

_____

_____

_____

_____

_____

_____

_____

_____

_____

_____

_____

_____

_____

_____

_____

_____

_____

What brings you the greatest happiness?

_____

_____

_____

_____

_____

_____

_____

_____

_____

_____

_____

_____

_____

_____

_____

_____

_____

_____

Week 7

Career

Our career choices are a very important part of
our lives. Most of us try to select a career that
makes us happy. This week, reflect on your
career choice as you go through your week and
journal about your satisfaction in regard to this
choice. If you find yourself unsatisfied, discuss
what you can do to fix that.

_____

_____

_____

_____

_____

_____

_____

_____

_____

_____

_____

_____

_____

_____

Week 8

Drive

As you go about your week, pay attention to the things throughout the day that keep you pushing forward. What drives you?

_____

_____

_____

_____

_____

_____

_____

_____

_____

_____

_____

_____

_____

_____

_____

_____

Week 9

What is YOUR story?

_____

_____

_____

_____

_____

_____

_____

_____

_____

_____

_____

_____

_____

_____

_____

_____

_____

_____

_____

_____

_____

_____

_____

Week 10
Availability

How available do you make yourself to others?
Do you expect others to be more available to you
than you are in return?

_____

_____

_____

_____

_____

_____

_____

_____

_____

_____

_____

_____

_____

_____

_____

_____

_____

Week 11
Strength

Where do you find your strength?

_____

_____

_____

_____

_____

_____

_____

_____

_____

_____

_____

_____

_____

_____

_____

_____

_____

_____

_____

_____

Week 12

What do you really wish others knew about you?

_____

_____

_____

_____

_____

_____

_____

_____

_____

_____

_____

_____

_____

_____

_____

_____

_____

_____

_____

_____

_____

_____

Week 13
Progression

Do you feel you are effectively progressing toward your goals? If not, what things can you do differently to get back on track? If so, discuss those goals and what you have done so far to stay on track.

_____

_____

_____

_____

_____

_____

_____

_____

_____

_____

_____

_____

_____

_____

_____

What things do you do that could hinder your progress?

_____

_____

_____

_____

_____

_____

_____

_____

_____

_____

_____

_____

_____

_____

_____

_____

_____

Week 14

Motivators

Who or what are your biggest motivators?

_____

_____

_____

_____

_____

_____

_____

_____

_____

_____

_____

_____

_____

_____

_____

_____

_____

_____

Are the things that motivate you based on negativity or positivity? For example: Are you motivated because someone said you couldn't do something? Or, are you motivated because people expect wonderful things from you?

_____

_____

_____

_____

_____

_____

_____

_____

_____

_____

_____

_____

_____

_____

_____

_____

_____

Week 15

What things or people are you taking for granted?

_____

_____

_____

_____

_____

_____

_____

_____

_____

_____

_____

_____

_____

_____

_____

_____

_____

_____

_____

_____

_____

_____

Week 16
Things that Hinder

Allowing things or people into our lives that hinder us can significantly stall us from getting where we need to be. What things do you allow to hinder you?

_____

_____

_____

_____

_____

_____

_____

_____

_____

_____

_____

_____

_____

_____

_____

_____

Week 17
Sadness

What thing(s) bring you the greatest sadness?

_____

_____

_____

_____

_____

_____

_____

_____

_____

_____

_____

_____

_____

_____

_____

_____

_____

_____

_____

_____

_____

How well do you handle moments of sadness?

_____

_____

_____

_____

_____

_____

_____

_____

_____

_____

_____

_____

_____

_____

_____

_____

_____

_____

_____

Week 18

What do you think it means to be true to yourself?

_____
_____
_____
_____
_____
_____
_____
_____
_____
_____
_____
_____
_____
_____
_____
_____
_____
_____
_____
_____
_____

Do you do the things you described? Why or why not?

_____

_____

_____

_____

_____

_____

_____

_____

_____

_____

_____

_____

_____

_____

_____

_____

_____

_____

_____

Week 19
Quitting

There are times we consider quitting, either because things become too hard or because something takes too long to happen. What things have you quit that you now wish you hadn't?

_____

_____

_____

_____

_____

_____

_____

_____

_____

_____

_____

_____

_____

_____

_____

_____

_____

_____

_____

_____

_____

_____

_____

Can quitting birth a positive outcome? Explain.

_____

_____

_____

_____

_____

_____

_____

_____

_____

_____

Week 20
What do you need?

In life, we all need something. Whether it be a loved one, a child, a memory, etc. What things do you need in life? What do these things do for you?

_____

_____

_____

_____

_____

_____

_____

_____

_____

_____

_____

_____

_____

_____

_____

If you were to lose any of these things, how would that affect you?

_____

_____

_____

_____

_____

_____

_____

_____

_____

_____

_____

_____

_____

_____

_____

_____

_____

_____

_____

Week 21

Are you giving your best effort?

We have to exhibit effort in almost every aspect of our lives for them to be successful. Whether it is a relationship, a job, etc. They all require our effort. How do you exhibit effort in these aspects of life:

Work:

_____

_____

_____

_____

_____

_____

Love:

_____

_____

_____

_____

_____

Friendships:

_____

_____

_____

_____

_____

_____

_____

_____

Career:

_____

_____

_____

_____

_____

_____

_____

_____

_____

_____

Week 22
Gratefulness

What are you most grateful for?

_____

_____

_____

_____

_____

_____

_____

_____

_____

_____

_____

_____

_____

_____

_____

_____

_____

_____

_____

Week 23
Goal Setting

How often do you set goals for yourself? How do you determine if something is important enough to set a goal for it?

_____

_____

_____

_____

_____

_____

_____

_____

_____

_____

_____

_____

_____

_____

_____

_____

_____

How successful have you been at achieving the goals you have set out for yourself? Discuss some successes and failures of previous goals.

_____

_____

_____

_____

_____

_____

_____

_____

_____

_____

_____

_____

_____

_____

_____

_____

_____

_____

_____

Week 24

I couldn't image living without.....

_____
_____
_____
_____
_____
_____
_____
_____
_____
_____
_____
_____
_____
_____
_____
_____
_____
_____
_____
_____
_____
_____

Week 25
Mistakes

Mistakes cause us to experience many different feelings, and can affect the people closest to us. Think over some of the biggest mistakes you've made and reflect on how they affected you and/or others.

_____

_____

_____

_____

_____

_____

_____

_____

_____

_____

_____

_____

_____

_____

_____

_____

Week 26

What valuable lessons have you learned about life?

_____

_____

_____

_____

_____

_____

_____

_____

_____

_____

_____

_____

_____

_____

_____

_____

_____

_____

_____

_____

_____

_____

Week 27

What are your biggest personal milestones?

_____

_____

_____

_____

_____

_____

_____

_____

_____

_____

_____

_____

_____

_____

_____

_____

_____

_____

_____

_____

_____

_____

Week 28

Finances

How well do you manage your finances?

_____

_____

_____

_____

_____

_____

_____

_____

_____

_____

_____

_____

_____

_____

_____

_____

_____

_____

_____

_____

_____

What financial mistakes have you made that taught you a lesson?

_____

_____

_____

_____

_____

_____

_____

_____

What steps have you made to either help you grow your finances or manage your finances better?

_____

_____

_____

_____

_____

_____

_____

_____

Week 29

Passion

Our passion is typically something that brings us pleasure. What is your greatest passion and how do you nurture it?

_____

_____

_____

_____

_____

_____

_____

_____

_____

_____

_____

_____

_____

_____

_____

_____

_____

Week 30

My first love is......

_____

_____

_____

_____

_____

_____

_____

_____

_____

_____

_____

_____

_____

_____

_____

_____

_____

_____

_____

_____

_____

Week 31
Greatest Moments

Our greatest moments are the things that have the greatest impacts on us. They are different than milestones because milestones are growth based. Your greatest moments are experiences. What are your greatest moments and how have they impacted your life?

_____

_____

_____

_____

_____

_____

_____

_____

_____

_____

_____

_____

_____

_____

_____

Week 32

Discovery

Reflect on things you have discovered about yourself as you mature. Do these things affect how you view yourself?

_____

_____

_____

_____

_____

_____

_____

_____

_____

_____

_____

_____

_____

_____

_____

Week 33

Certain things are completely out of our control, however, we still worry about them. What things do you worry about that you can't control and why?

_____

_____

_____

_____

_____

_____

_____

_____

_____

_____

_____

_____

_____

_____

_____

_____

_____

Week 34

How well do you keep promises to yourself and others?

_____
_____
_____
_____
_____
_____
_____
_____
_____
_____
_____
_____
_____
_____
_____
_____
_____
_____
_____
_____
_____
_____
_____
_____

Week 35
Opportunities

We have all been faced with opportunities. As you go through the week, pay attention to any opportunities that present themselves, whether they are personally or professionally. Discuss how you will manage those opportunities.

_____

_____

_____

_____

_____

_____

_____

_____

_____

_____

_____

_____

_____

_____

Week 36

How well are you currently balancing life?

_____

_____

_____

_____

_____

_____

_____

_____

_____

_____

_____

_____

_____

_____

_____

_____

_____

_____

_____

_____

_____

_____

_____

_____

_____

Week 37

Compassion

How have you showed compassion for the people in your life?

_____

_____

_____

_____

_____

_____

_____

_____

_____

_____

_____

_____

_____

_____

_____

_____

_____

_____

_____

Do you feel your family, friends or loved ones are compassionate with you? Why or why not?

_____

_____

_____

_____

_____

_____

_____

_____

_____

_____

_____

_____

_____

_____

_____

_____

_____

_____

Week 38
Communication

The way we communicate is often how people view us. How well do you think you communicate?

_____

_____

_____

_____

_____

_____

_____

_____

_____

_____

_____

_____

_____

_____

_____

_____

_____

_____

How is your communication when you are angry/
hurt/disappointed?

_____

_____

_____

_____

_____

_____

_____

_____

_____

_____

Has someone mentioned you don't communicate
well? What can you do to improve that?

_____

_____

_____

_____

_____

_____

_____

_____

Week 39

Generosity

You can be generous with your time, money, etc. What does generosity mean to you?

_____

_____

_____

_____

_____

_____

_____

_____

_____

_____

_____

_____

_____

_____

_____

_____

_____

Do you feel you are too generous or not generous enough? Explain.

_____

_____

_____

_____

_____

_____

_____

_____

_____

_____

_____

_____

_____

_____

_____

_____

_____

_____

_____

Week 40

Confidence

How confident do you feel about who you are?

_____

_____

_____

_____

_____

_____

_____

_____

_____

_____

_____

_____

_____

_____

_____

_____

_____

_____

_____

_____

What situations do you feel you're most confident in?

_____

_____

_____

_____

_____

_____

_____

_____

_____

_____

_____

_____

_____

_____

_____

_____

_____

_____

_____

Week 41
Self Identity

How do you see yourself? (Are you a good person, a positive person, etc.)

_____
_____
_____
_____
_____
_____
_____
_____

Do you think others view you the same way you view yourself?

_____
_____
_____
_____
_____
_____
_____

Are there things you would like to change about
the way others may view you? If so, what are they?

_____

_____

_____

_____

_____

_____

_____

_____

_____

_____

_____

_____

_____

_____

_____

_____

_____

_____

_____

Week 42

Inspiration

What inspires you most? Why?

_____

_____

_____

_____

_____

_____

_____

_____

_____

_____

_____

_____

_____

_____

_____

_____

_____

Who inspires you most? How?

_____

_____

_____

_____

_____

_____

_____

_____

_____

_____

_____

_____

_____

_____

_____

_____

_____

_____

_____

Week 43

Forgiveness

Forgiveness can be hard, especially when we are hurting. How good are you at forgiving others when their actions hurt you?

_____

_____

_____

_____

_____

_____

_____

_____

_____

_____

_____

_____

_____

_____

_____

_____

_____

_____

Have there been times you have had to ask for forgiveness? How did that make you feel?

_____

_____

_____

_____

_____

_____

_____

_____

_____

_____

_____

_____

_____

_____

_____

_____

_____

_____

Do you think there is an expectation that you have to forgive someone simply because they apologize? Why or why not?

_____

_____

_____

_____

_____

_____

_____

_____

_____

_____

_____

_____

_____

_____

_____

_____

_____

Week 44
Dependability

Your dependability says a lot about your character. Do you consider yourself a dependable person? Explain.

_____

_____

_____

_____

_____

_____

_____

_____

_____

_____

_____

_____

_____

_____

_____

_____

Do you think those closest to you would consider you dependable? Why or why not?

_____

_____

_____

_____

_____

_____

_____

_____

_____

_____

_____

_____

_____

_____

_____

_____

_____

_____

Week 45
Self Control

How well do you handle yourself in situations that make you angry, sad, excited, etc.?

_____

_____

_____

_____

_____

_____

_____

_____

_____

_____

_____

_____

_____

_____

_____

_____

_____

Week 46
Pain

Pain can come in many shapes and forms. Physical pain seems to leave our minds when we are alleviated from it; however, emotional pain seems to stick with us for a significant period of time. What things have brought you the greatest pain and how did you manage it?

_____

_____

_____

_____

_____

_____

_____

_____

_____

_____

_____

_____

_____

_____

Week 47
Support

List the people who genuinely support you and what role they play.

_____

_____

_____

_____

_____

_____

_____

_____

Do you provide the same support for others, that you expect from them?

_____

_____

_____

_____

_____

_____

_____

Have you ever expected support from someone and didn't get it. How did that affect you?

_____

_____

_____

_____

_____

_____

_____

_____

_____

_____

_____

_____

_____

_____

_____

_____

_____

_____

Week 48

Promises to self

What 10 promises have you made to yourself that you NEED to keep?

_____

_____

_____

_____

_____

_____

_____

_____

_____

_____

_____

_____

_____

_____

_____

_____

_____

_____

_____

Week 49
What hurts now?

What things are you emotionally dealing with right now?

_____

_____

_____

_____

_____

_____

_____

_____

_____

_____

_____

_____

_____

_____

_____

_____

_____

_____

Week 50
Talent

What are your greatest talents and how do you nurture them?

_____

_____

_____

_____

_____

_____

_____

_____

_____

_____

_____

_____

_____

_____

_____

_____

Has anyone ever said you are wasting your talents? Do you agree? Why or why not?

_____

_____

_____

_____

_____

_____

_____

_____

_____

_____

_____

_____

_____

_____

_____

_____

_____

_____

_____

_____

Week 51

Advice

Do you seek advice often? If so, who do you typically seek advice from and why?

_____

_____

_____

_____

_____

_____

_____

_____

_____

_____

_____

_____

_____

_____

_____

_____

_____

_____

How good are you at taking your own advice?

_____

_____

_____

_____

_____

_____

_____

_____

_____

_____

_____

_____

_____

_____

_____

_____

_____

_____

_____

Week 52

Doors

What doors are you glad didn't open for you?
Why?

_____

_____

_____

_____

_____

_____

_____

_____

_____

_____

_____

_____

_____

_____

_____

_____

_____

_____

_____

What's Next For You?

_____

_____

_____

_____

_____

_____

_____

_____

_____

_____

_____

_____

_____

_____

_____

_____

_____

_____

_____

_____

_____

About The Author

Erika is an author, freelance writer, blogger; owner of It's Only Write Communications, and most importantly, a mom. Erika has spent the past II years writing and contributing for several print and online publications. She's set her focus on encouraging and motivating others to pursue their dreams through self-discovery.

For more information about the author please visit: www.erikardawkins.com